Kenet
Margaret

14.10.10

SWEET SONGS FROM THE HEART

Nthatheni Kenneth Nengovhela was born in 1966 in Dzwerani, Mahematshena village. He taught in his local secondary school from 1986 to 1987 and in 1988 he enrolled at the Thohoyandou Nursing Campus. He completed his studies in 1991 and gained a Diploma in Nursing Science (General, Psychiatric and Community) and Midwifery. He is presently staying in the West Midlands, England.

"In the early stages of this book, there were many times of frustration, anger, desperation and indecisiveness. But through self-confidence, I managed to overcome these obstacles. I have moved from the dark to the wonderful light so that I can be seen, and this was no easy task. This collection of poetry was written especially for you so that it may provoke your emotions and thoughts and let you rediscover aspects of life. These poems (songs) were written with my greatest love and respect for individuals."

SWEET SONGS FROM THE HEART

Nthatheni Kenneth Nengovhela

ARTHUR H. STOCKWELL LTD.
Torrs Park   Ilfracombe   Devon
Established 1898
www.ahstockwell.co.uk

British Library Cataloguing-in-Publication Data.
A catalogue record for this book is available
from the British Library.

Dedication

To my very bosom friend and wife, Funanani Hildah,
lovely kids Khathutshelo Lufunoand Pfariso Nadia.

ISBN 0 7223 3561-X
Printed in Great Britain by
Arthur H. Stockwell Ltd.
Torrs Park   Ilfracombe
Devon

Acknowledgements

I would like to forward my acknowledgements to the following individuals; Bernard N. Netangaheni, my close friend who was so inspirational in the early stages of the project and who criticised me in most of the songs, and for his views which prompted me to change and rearrange some of the songs. Nnditsheni Ravele, my brother and friend, who took the initiative in encouraging me and challenging me to put my work into a book for the majority to sing and to light up the 'hidden talent' in me, after I had sung two songs during his departure from our choir. He was a stimulus that has prepared me to be mentally and physically prepared in a task so great.

Pandelani, a classmate and a friend, who was always pestering me to come out of my shell and work for excellence as he believed in my experiments.

My deepest gratitude goes to Konanani Manenzhe who took her time in proofreading the entire manuscript and cross questioned me why I have written this and not that, and the aims of the songs.

Mr Gideon Nesengani, whom I regard an advisor par excellence as he had discussed with me the finer points of working towards success and to guard oneself against complacency and ruthless haste that could retard the development of the book.

Louise Dawson, a friend who was so inspirational and

loved what I hadbeen trying to achieve.

Again I would love to say "Thank you very much" to Mr Selwyn Lewis and family (Cape Town) who had contributed a lot in making this book get published.

My family members, who have silently encouraged me, wished and longed for the safe arrival of their newborn, Sweet Songs from the Heart ...

Words are not enough
Actions may not be impressive
Gold I do not have
To thank you all
In your invaluable
And greatest contributions
You have made.

12.11.1997

Contents

Dear Mother And Father   9

Elephants   10

Drought   12

Conflicts   13

The Song   14

My Africa   15

The Poor Fellow And The Rich Man   16

The Dead Man   17

The Prisoner   18

Your Pains   19

The Pool   20

Loneliness   21

Hostage   22

Extra   23

Colours   24

Buried Emotions   25

The Yes Man   26

Let Him Breathe   27

He Believes   28

Exhausted Love   29

Metals   30

Want To Be Rich   31

SOS   32

This Noise   33

Farewell To A Colleague   34

Reasons To Marry   36

I Wish I Were A Fish   37

Over The River   38

The Stone   39

The Mother's Wish   40

The Creators   41

Death   42

The Couple   43

Human Body   44

Directions   45

The Journey   46

He...y Halt   47

Watching The Maize Grow   48

Dear Mother And Father

He is the effort of your struggle
But he must not be maimed by snipers.
He did not ask to be born
Nor did you ask to bear him.

You were forced to unite love
By the wisdom of the ancestors' law.
They mentioned not they coerced you
To swim joyfully creature infested oceans.

You were fumigated with hatred
And you jogged chest-high either way
Leaving a trail of weeping manikins,
With no trophy to display.

Now you meet under the moonlight.
In your love-hatred the moon has no light
It leaves you in pitch-dark alleys.
In your hiding the sight is Halley's Comet.

Mother and Father, life is bittersweet,
So make use of its sweetness
And throw the bitterness in butter pot
For the sake of his embryonic cycle.

Elephants

Elephants adore each other;
When the other big one dies
They trumpet in unison
Raising their trunks to heaven
As if trying to sing to God.

Elephants have eyes for themselves
They forget the ants on the ground
They trample on them with dignity
And the ants die before their deaths
When giants frolic with no concern.

The elephants drink in a home pool
They drink until mud is left
They leave diverse species dying
Slow painful shameless deaths
And the elephants never saw anything.

The elephants break trees happily
Sending birds' homes flying high
Like parachutes in all directions
And they kill the future birds
Citing fair play as an answer.

Elephants are bloodsuckers
Elephants are harvesters
But they are lazy tillers
And they sow dead seeds,
But they are the world.

Elephants are big with no brains
They live for the present,
Ants are future strategists,
They are tiny with bigger brains
And they know times of troubles.

Elephants are Goliaths in armour,
Ants are Davids in feathers,
But none is to shiver and die
As they are involved in a mock battle,
It is part of their endless daily ration.

Drought

Water flows down the river for good
It increases the intensity of heat.
The sun scrapes the flesh.
The flesh gives way to expose the skeleton.

The skeletons seem happy to laugh together
Lying down hiding the whole day.
It is the aftermath of drought;
Who survive will tell the story.

The drought has eaten all the animals,
It has confiscated all the grazing land
Leaving everybody stunned with terror
As if waiting to be a prey.

Drought invades with all its deadly arrows.
It shoots to kill living things.
Its regiments are invincible.
It smelts steel like a furnace.

The drought eats all stored food;
The earth refuses all seeds;
Men bend down for good,
Their knees disobeying their orders.

Drought is truly merciless.
It does not show any respect.
It enters golden palaces of kings
And eats freshly picked fruits.

Conflicts

People abstain from feeding
And cook war for dinner,
Lacking constructive acts,
Pretending to be the best thinkers.

Hatred and distrust brew deadly beer,
People use their clever hands
Like a stick to irritate the wasps
And forget their disabled minds.

Spectators cry in amusement,
Fighters cry for speedy intervention;
The crowd want endless visual snacks
To down them with red spring water.

The fighters have no blankets
That bring the warmth of love,
As they have chased the spy of love
And invited the enemy that drinks love.

The conflict has no love
As it lacks hospitality and peace.
Whenever love starts fire
Conflicts pour in ice-cold water.

The Song

If the song
You sing
Is the song
I sing,
Why do not we sing together
To make the tone better?
So we bring it in tune
With the sounds of the waterfalls
And pair it with raindrops
That fall on my ancient drums.

My Africa

I prepared my baggage at Cape of Good Hope,
I sailed the air to Senegal;
In Morocco I took a nice nap,
In Tunisia I refreshed myself with ice;
I reached Somalia during supper,
In Mozambique I saw kids playing joyfully,
Then I silently returned to my Cape.

My Africa, your parents have divorced,
Your mother has rolled to the west,
Your father did sprint to the east;
You are an orphan of your living parents,
Now they peep through your windows
Lusting after your exposed wealth.
Now tell me who are your parents?

Your angelic beauty frustrates them;
Mt Kilimanjaro leaves them agape;
They kill the wild as if herding them,
They all have twin minds;
They wanted to destroy your being,
They pretend to love their only child,
They are after your precious stones.

Father gives you guns to kill Mother,
Mother gives you guns to destroy Father.
Now tell me who are your parents?
Your parents want to cut your neck
Waiting at a distance as if blind;
My Africa, be on the lookout
Otherwise they will sink you in the ocean.

The Poor Fellow And The Rich Man

The poor man stabbed the rich man,
It makes headline news,
The fellow wants to step up the ladder.
The rich man killed the poor fellow
And it is a regrettable accident,
But he was standing in danger's way.

The fellow tries to enrich himself
Through his God-given skills,
He is branded a thief, taking from the man;
The rich man's potbelly is now small,
He is being sucked by the poor fellow,
But the fellow is still skin and bones.

The poor fellow hates the rich man;
The fellow and the man will never sup together,
The fellow is a stain on a pure white cloth;
The man proclaims himself God,
He fears nothing that stands on legs,
His only worry is a gang of fellows.

The poor fellow waters the rich man,
He becomes a green gigantic boabab
In a sea of dying furnace-hot sand;
The fellow moils and toils from here to there
Until he saw his face on the floor
Making it ready for the noon waltz.

The poor man is flesh and blood,
The rich man is no different from him,
They all walk on the same barren earth,
They all breathe in the same oxygen,
But the rich man fears the advent of the poor
As they will consume all the oxygen
And the man will die the poor fellow's death.

The Dead Man

He has divorced the first life
He has married the life of the dead;
I wonder if you remember him,
He lived and vanished like vapour.
He has been put to rest,
The way you comfort him.

He lived a poor man's life,
He had no real true friend
Save those who share his sufferings.
Now people throng from far and near
To see the dead man's burial
And put him in his resting place.

I wonder if he needs rest,
He used to wander many miles
Scavenging for anything to eat,
He became weary and dehydrated
But nobody gave him an armchair,
Now they insist he really needs rest.

I wonder if they needed him,
They put him face down
In the casket for a prince,
They locked it with double hard steel
They put tons of gravel over him,
They seal with triple hard concrete.

If he is half dead in the grave
He had played a sure wrong trick,
His move is measured in the box,
He won't remove the concrete lid;
What he must sincerely know is
Out of sight is out of mind of the living.

The Prisoner

I admire your personality
I wish it were a cloth
That you can pass on to me
And I give pieces to all
So everybody can have a share.

That time we parted ways
You did not narrate all to me,
I forgot to bid you goodbye
As your mouth was chained
And you were made to sit on razor blades.

Your words were of constructive love
That sent deadly gas to all,
They labelled you an evil man,
They set their beasts free
To graze on your mielie fields.

You called a thief by his trade
And he painfully hamstrung you,
He put hot pepper in your eyes,
And he forced you to tell lies
But you remained an unrepentant devil.

Everything comes to an end;
I will be glad when you are set free
And your sleep highly blessed.
Like a ship I will sail your freedom,
You leaving everything to Nature.

Your Pains

Your pains are mine
As mine are yours
And you are mine,
We are united in pains,
The pains of labour.

You laid a golden egg
That you did not see,
As somebody put the snake's egg
In your laying nest
Therefore you will hatch a snake.

Your golden egg is mine,
That snake's chick is yours only,
You chose not to hatch a snake
But you warm its egg
Thinking it was really yours.

You loved not to hatch a serpent,
It didn't like to be yours.
It was a conflict during birth,
That had destroyed your golden time
As your hatching was made difficult.

Your pains are mine
My pains are yours
And you are mine,
We are united in pains,
The pains of love.

The Pool

Its water is night dark,
Its water is dead quiet,
Its source is far from naked eyes;
This pool sits comfortably among trees
Contemplating its future among trees.

Its water is an unusually quiet bride;
Below it lie merciless beasts
That roam the bottom boastfully
Waiting for those overwhelmed with temptations
So they can strike a fatal blow.

The pool lies leisurely singing its praises,
It invites uninvited guests for dinner;
This is to set a deadly trap;
It calls its huge bravest men
To dine and protect its sovereignty.

What is below is hidden;
The roots are thorns and needles;
They prick feet and you're dead
Moaning of excruciating pains;
The pool itself smiling mockingly.

Do fish live in its water?
Yes, they seem to live above water
As below is frightening hellfire;
The pool living in hell and ice,
Mimicking both lives below and above.

Loneliness

He is a lone hawker,
Alone in his place of torment;
Selling his wares to an invisible crowd,
He beckoned it with both hands shaking
For it to share his burden of poverty;
Alone he stands lonely longing for company.
His loneliness is shared by his double self,
He lacks a body to energise him
As his selves are gagged for life;
Loneliness wards off his would-be soothers,
As it bares its peace-piercing teeth;
Loneliness is a true friend of himself,
It captures him to be so lonely; so lonely;
Loneliness grows to less and less life
Until it pins him down due to his folly.

Hostage

The world lives in the cocoon,
The outside is gripped by fear,
The fear that threatens the feared
Filling the inner chamber with hostages.

The world lives in a concrete house,
The house is surrounded by titanium.
The best marksmen are put on top
To destroy every fear on sight.

Even great men live in prisons,
They are reluctantly taken hostage;
They are also encapsulated by fast men
Who have threads, extra ears and bulging sticks.

The world is oppressed by its fear,
Everybody lives in a darkened cocoon,
The outside is only safe to God,
The dead are half safe before desecration.

The world is a hostage,
The ransom is going up hourly,
There is a nice match now
And mismatch two hours to follow.

The world is a hostage,
It lives between boxed lines,
If it attempts to move it's gone
Under the hammer that crushes to crunchies.

The world lives in the cocoon,
The world lives in concrete shelters,
The shelters that house great men,
Fearsome great men who are hostages.

Extra

True honey is extra sweet,
It adds vigour to the body;
Diluted honey is less sweet,
It is unpalatable to hungry tongues;
Peppered honey is extra hot,
It cuts the dying tongues;
It removes the moving ears,
It is extra sweet and extra hot;
Bribed honey sweats and it haunts;
Watered honey is cactus juice,
It is extra sticky, prickly and watery;
When dry it is extra hard,
Extra sweet is extra salivation,
Extra hot is watery eyes.

Colours

White is for pure joy,
White is for clear victory,
White is for real purity;
Black is for real death,
Black is for real evil;
Red is for the coming danger,
Red is for the assassin.

You wear black you're mourning,
You wear white you're over the moon,
Brides wear white for the joy of the wedding;
You raised the white flag,
You have won the peace battle;
You see the danger red,
You stop and quickly retreat.

You call the colour black
But it is not evil or dead,
You call the other colour white
But it has neither of the characteristics;
All beings have red blood, I suppose;
Only insects have black and white blood,
Black, white and red are beings with blood.

Colours are man's cruel imaginations,
Colours are man's heaven and earth,
Colours are man's misfit weapons;
When colours are air and mist
They are carried in black boxes,
They are silently moved in black limousines,
But they are locked inside the red earth.

Buried Emotions

He should have laughed
But he was unable;
He should have cried
But he was unable;
He should have received love
But there was nobody to offer it.

He should have grown to be a man
But he remains a hapless child;
He should have asked questions
But he kept cool and quiet;
He should have strongly disagreed
But he quietly assented with anger inside.

When he wants to laugh
He cries with tears of joy and sorrow;
When he wants to cry
His heart is torn into bits;
When he wants to think good
He finds himself wooing bad.

Does God have a say in real life?
Is he the one to control his destiny?
It seems he is the main switch,
The battered living on borrowed time;
He grumbles about the tense past,
His present is down, his future is healthy.

The Yes Man

Do you know English?
Yes, sir.
Do you know French?
Oh yes, sir.
Do you know Greek?
Yes, sir; he nodded.
Can you talk in all these?
Yes, sir.
Go on, my man.
English is my father.
French is my mother.
Greek is my sister.
Irish is me.
My father knows England.
I know Irish shores.
Jill has knowledge of Greece;
Mama is Madame Sofronie.
I thought you can speak all these.
Yes, sir, yes, sir.
Are you sure?
As sure as death, sir.
Are you serious, little boy?
Yes, Sir MacAdam.

Let Him Breathe

They detest raw fish,
It is nice when cooked,
It smells and nauseates when raw,
But the end action is filling the gut.

If you do and harm nobody
Get pleasure through your moves.

Remove zigzag racial lines
That retard the leaves' growth.

Have room for the great differences;
As humans are scattered stones
None of it can be compared to the other.

Nobody must construct a tarred road
Over other people's fountains of life,
They must be given breathing space.

Let us do what we do
But no killing please,
Let him breathe another day.

He Believes

He believes in love,
He believes in peace,
He believes in unity,
He believes in human life.

His beliefs are genuine,
In his corner of isolation;
He reaches out for somebody
But everybody calls him a madman.

His beliefs are perfect,
His beliefs are in the masses,
If his beliefs are invisible
Then the world is his friend.

He believes in sharing love,
He believes in firing war,
But he fights a lone battle
Like a cat chasing its shadow.

He believes in Nature
As we all believe in Nature
And Nature believes in the Supreme
That had survived all wars.

He believes in love,
He believes in human prosperity,
The world agrees on peace and happiness
When we believe in bonding love.

Exhausted Love

Her grannies have taught her
To love them dearly,
To love her parents endlessly,
To love her God wholeheartedly,
To love her toys and pets dearly,
To love her siblings with no exception.

They never told her
To have room for hatred,
To hate in self-defence,
To hate for survival,
To hate to be humane,
To hate to have selfless adoration.

Now she wants to love dearly,
The inborn instincts are gone.
Love has waned in her development.
Nobody wants to give her love
Everybody needs her love.
Her love has passed its peak already,
Her exhausted love has flown home.

Metals

A metalful idiot:
>   is god,
>   is King,
>   is Strong,
>   is Powerful.

The other idiot:
>   is Grave,
>   is Air,
>   is Trash,
>   is Mouthless.

Metals are saps' vehicles.

Want To Be Rich?

Declare the global air we breathe is your property,
Sell this gold at one rand per person per week for life.

SOS

No brakes,
Tank is fuelless;
Hooves are durable,
Speed is supersonic;
No stopping,
The tar is downhill;
Disaster is probable,
Please lend a hand.

This Noise

This piece of noise and that piece of noise
When chiselled they are honey
That sweeten the ears and the soul
Leaving the toes tingling with sweet moves.

This noise brings tranquillity to the heart,
It pumps blood to the head
Keeping the hair at the right angle
And bringing fear to the whole body
Through its indoctrinating lessons.

This noise sends you in a trance
And you see good people of Mars
Who beckoned you to change life,
You willingly followed the signs
Then you explode with euphoria.

This noise is highly contagious
No cure, no comfort but death and death
But it will not get enough of us,
It loves very tenderly
And it kills very softly.

This noise reminds me of Bangui,
It plants me in my genuine roots;
It brings pieces of peace to all,
This piece of noise is here for good,
It is a saviour and destroyer of self.

Farewell To A Colleague

Farewell ain't really well indeed,
It is hidden anger and sorrow
That we avoid to put in the mirror
As it seems childish to be in truth.

It pains us to be weaned prematurely,
We were sharing the same breasts,
The painful breasts of anguish and humility
That stressed our energy to the limit.

You worked odd hours like an ass,
Your master was born blind and deaf;
He hid behind Flora and her call
To suppress your desire to be others
Who get rands through their breathings.

You were a master of your assumed trade,
You were joy and laughter to all trades;
You have love, humour, compassion and discipline,
These are no mock exaggerations dear friend
But true attributes from fragile bosoms,
Attributes truly fitting for your head.

You have chased your successor,
Leaving a hollow empty throne
That nobody will love to think of
As it will bring death pains to all
And a choir of sobs and weepings.

Let us give you 'bye cheers,
Cheers of longevity and prosperity
As you cycle to the true north,
We cherish your going with luck.

This is the right time to evaporate
To places of green pastures
Where you eat with tears of pride and joy,
The joy that quenches your thirst to advance.

You must follow Him who leads
In all your solo expeditions;
Hurry to collect your golden cup
Before cheaters can claim it
And you remain a worthless adventurer.

Reasons To Marry

If you marry real Mary
You will have a merry life;
And you marry Crestine
Life will be an uphill battle.

You marry for beauty
And beauties are few,
More souls will flock to beauty
Like flies to a dead carcass.

You marry to sire offspring,
They will be a yoke on your neck,
And you scold the day of your birth
As you oppose their will for freedom.

You marry for pure pleasure
And you forget that pleasure is dew,
It vanishes with sunrise
And you remain dry and dying.

You marry as your father did;
He is the culprit and victim of abuse,
And you want to follow suit
Like sheep to a slaughterhouse.

You marry for comfort and shelter,
Comfort then turns to prickling pains
That tear your heart to shreds
And you wish you were born a tree.

You marry as God has given you
One to enjoy the bliss of life with,
You will wish to live twice
As death will give you pure sadness.

I Wish I Were A Fish

I wish I were a river fish,
I would have not been eating gall;
Leaving golden honey to go bitter
And leaving my mouth foul-smelling,
And choosing to suffer in the universe
And eating with tears streaming down my face.

I wish I were a river fish
That never goes hungry even with no job;
It eats to its stomach's brim
Though it never stores in silos,
And it never carries a killing gun
As it lives peacefully with its friends.

I wish I were a river fish
That never constructs segregating lines,
It goes up and down the river peacefully
Without any need for devilish papers.
I wish we can change to chameleons
And stalk the fish in its climactic life.

Over The River

Nobody goes over the river,
They say there are beasts
That devour anything fleshy
Leaving bones for juicy melting soup;
These carnivores fear not the honourables.

Nobody goes over the river,
The daredevils are not yet back;
Those who follow are in coma,
It frightens even the jet-fighters,
They cross only on a one-way ticket.

There is darkness over the river
That intimidates the enemy;
Those who cross over are blind,
Their ears are immune to deafening sounds
As they are playing in the epicentre.

The love that helps you to cross over
Is the love that puts life over the river;
Some say life is excellent over there,
Some say life is excellent over here,
To know you must be a shining star.

The Stone

The stone cut his sleep,
It shatters the panes;
They scatter in tatters
Falling on his scattered hair
On the head that lay still;
Like steel there was noise,
Still he lay still on his steel;
Worriedly they give him consciousness,
Still he lay coldly still;
He is now a cold still steel,
The stone has cut his nice sleep still.

The Mother's Wish

Sometimes he is a boy,
Sometimes she is a girl,
But she must not be a girl-boy;
Their manoeuvres are deceiving.

He kicks like a hungry striker,
She dances like a slim ballerina;
The mother wishes he is a boy
To sustain the dying line.

In two weeks you will be out,
Taking contaminated air like others;
You will cry to get attention;
You will cease to breathe mechanically.

You are going to respect the mother
As doctors respect human beings,
And engineers sympathise with technology;
The mother wishes you to be the best.

You must grow to respect your mother,
You must grow to love your siblings,
You must be there when they cry,
Be compassionate enough to be them.

Do not make her heart bleed
Through your learned behaviours,
That can declare you a beast,
A beast fit to be shot dead.

The Creators

They create to avoid sorrow,
They create to mask reality,
They create to appease desires,
They create to leave their prints.

They bring life to dead souls,
They hasten the deaths of the ill,
They plant laughter in deaf-mutes,
They are magnificent in their trade.

The creators are bored to death,
They die silent deaths and live,
Leaving sorrow in spasms of words
And bake a puzzle of confused creation.

Creators are clever and amusing,
They spend their energy weaving
A web of intelligent crooked lines
That hoist them above the masters.

The creators bring joy to drunken hearts,
At times they smother thoughts to nothing,
Creating their inventions from nowhere
And keep them sailing the world over.

Creators are double clever and super stupid,
They create a wonderful world of dreams,
Fantasising and living happily in vacuum
And present red roses from their thrones.

Death

It strikes very slowly,
In crisis it acts swiftly;
It is a criminal on the list.
It robs us of sweet morrow,
It kissed us prematurely,
It cuts our bodies short,
It is a thief of various tricks.
It took him in his sleep,
He tried to kick but missed.
She met him on her wedding.
He was proud to be her man.
He makes himself global laws
That are meted out with no mercy
To children of defenceless parents.

The Couple

The wrinkled couple is over the top;
Biology did not dampen their faith;
They yearned for any child
But only from their faith.

Unbelievable but true to the core,
The couple got their last wish,
A bouncy little innocent boy,
Thanks Nature is no man's friend.

The boy was their god,
The boy was their parents,
He rolled without knowing their desire,
Their desire to be teenage parents.

The second set of teeth was gold,
One by one they crowded the mouth;
The couple saw it as a miracle,
A miracle they couldn't be proud of.

Gold is scarce in villages,
A piece of gold is needed by each villager;
If they pluck out his entire wealth,
He will not be a lovely rich man.

Gold is worthless when stored;
It fetches high price in the market;
Must he sell his assets one by one,
To supplement his parents' poverty?

Thieves learnt of his wealth;
They killed him to sell his teeth,
They are caught before transactions;
The couple mourned bitterly for Goldboy.

The couple had no freedom of choice,
They got what they did not love;
A golden boy they did receive,
A golden boy they did lose.

Human Body

What a wonderful piece,
It is pure art,
It is a true perfection of beauty.

Human body is amazing,
Its beauty is seen in truth,
Its beauty is great in lies.

It is crooked like hoops,
It is straight like a needle,
In reality nobody can copy it.

Human body is a sponge,
Human body is a spring,
Its suppleness is of real clay.

Human body is dazzling in its entity,
It reflects the moon and the stars,
It pulls them to mother earth.

Human body is a rare artefact,
Produced by the master artisan
Who moulded it to its artistic model.

Its appendages are computer threads
That are universal know-alls,
Relying heavily on their master chip.

What a wonderful piece;
Human body is pure moving art,
The most beautiful art on earth.

Directions

East is west
When you are west,
West is east
When you are east,
Up is up
When you are down,
Down is down
When you are up,
It seems confusing,
Frustrating,
Boring,
Time-consuming,
Purposeless
And
Amateurish.
Isn't it?

The Journey

What a terrible blow
When this breath is blown to soap bubbles,
Moving up to scatter sad messages,
To those below looking with hand-capped faces;
Hatred and sneer is printed all over their faces.

Members mentioned they wished to delay the flight,
Their wishes were no match to his desire;
He wanted the earth and hated heaven;
He was moved from pillar to post;
They knew not his skin is no heatproof.

He needed more of their brew
And more of it is lethal;
He then resigned to his deathbed,
His prayers were to be answered
As he lay motionless in attentive manner.

He attached his meaning to his cloth,
To them it secures, to him it expels demons;
He moved without a respectable parade,
It was a painful and inglorious farewell,
It was a shock and disgrace to his members.

They still look him in his young sinless face
With a striped cloth as a deadly tie.
Those who drank his gin never needed it at all,
They grumble he should have reached the sixth hour,
Powerless and guilty he departed in the third hour.

He....y Halt

Shoot to kill,
Leave no dead man standing,
Let no dead man crawls;
Advance swiftly and cunningly,
Blast everything movable,
Trees and animals are the greatest threat,
Raze them down,
Wait, watch the dust go down
And sing victory,
Glorifying God's name.

Watching The Maize Grow

It is a clot
Buried in the earth,
It sips invisible water,
It bursts after thirst;
It is magnificent to spectate.

The sprouts raise their heads,
They peep through the openings
And hold their hands for greeting,
This happens at lightning speed,
This is sheer magic to witness.

It camouflages itself
From snow to pure grass,
It stretches to the upper air,
It is a mountain from a hillock;
It grows taller when being spied.

It is now airborne,
It dwarfs the watcher pitifully,
It is now flowering
It has a nice goatee,
It is splendid to feast with it.

It is now a parent,
It has countless children,
It is dry and reburied,
It waits the deaths of kids,
It feels good to watch the maize grow.